COLLEGE FOOTBALL'S GREATEST RIVALRIES

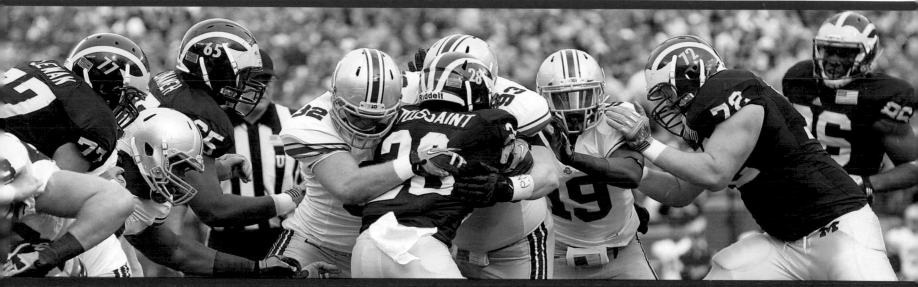

MICHIGAN vs. OHIO STATE

MATTHEW MONTEVERDE

press.

New York

Dedicated to Holly

Published in 2013 by The Rosen Publishing Group, Inc.
29 East 21st Street, New York, NY 10010

First Edition

Editor: Dean Galiano
Book Design: Dean Galiano and Matthew Monteverde

Photo Credits: Cover, Leon Halip/Getty Images, Gregory Shamus/Getty Images, G. N. Lowrance/Getty Images, p. 4 (background image) Diamond Images/Getty Images; p. 5 (background image) Leon Halip/Getty Images, Heinz Kluetmeier/Getty Images/Sports Illustrated; p. 7 Harry How/Getty Images; p. 9 David Maxwell/Getty Images; pp. 11 Associated Press; p. 13 Associated Press; p. 15 (inset) HeinzKluetmeier/Getty Images; p. 15 John Iacono/Getty Images/Sports Illustrated; p. 17 Gregory Shamus/Getty Images; p. 19 Kevin C. Cox/Getty Images; pp. 20-21 Jamie Sabau/Getty Images; p. 21 Elsa/Getty Images.

Library of Congress Cataloging-in-Publication Data

Monteverde, Matthew.
 Michigan vs. Ohio State / by Matthew Monteverde. -- 1st ed.
    p. cm. -- (College football's greatest rivalries)
 Includes index.
 ISBN 978-1-4777-1159-0 (library binding) -- ISBN 978-1-4777-1165-1 (pbk.) -- ISBN 978-1-4777-1166-8 (6-pack)
 1. University of Michigan--Football--History--Juvenile literature. 2. University of Michigan Wolverines- (Football team)--History--Juvenile literature. 3. Ohio State University--Football--History--Juvenile literature. 4. Ohio State Buckeyes (Football team)--History--Juvenile literature. I. Title.
 GV958.M5M66 2013
 796.332'630977--dc23
                                    2012042883

Manufactured in the United States of America

CPSIA Compliance Information: Batch #W13PKF: For Further Information contact Rosen Publishing, New York, New York at 1-800-237-9932

CONTENTS

THE BIRTH OF A RIVALRY

The Michigan versus Ohio State college football **rivalry** is one of the most famous matchups in sports. The two teams have faced each other more than 100 times since their first game in 1897. Their first game wasn't even close, as Michigan shut out Ohio State, 34-0. Since then, however, the rivalry has produced many close games.

One of the main reasons the two teams are rivals is because the University of Michigan and Ohio State University are located in **neighboring** states. In addition, each team plays in the same college football **conference**, called the Big Ten. Each year millions of people across the country watch Michigan and Ohio State battle it out on the football field. Their **annual** football game has become so well known that it has its own nickname: "The Game."

Michigan and Ohio State play each other every year. Here, the teams battle it out during the 1976 game in front of a packed house at Ohio Stadium. The stadium is also called The Horseshoe due to its shape.

THE MICHIGAN WOLVERINES

The University of Michigan's football team is known as the Wolverines. They play their home games at Michigan Stadium, located in Ann Arbor, Michigan. The Wolverines have a long and rich football history. They played their first game in 1879. Since then, the Wolverine football team has won 11 national championships. The Wolverines won their most recent championship in 1997.

Many of the Wolverine's top football players have gone on to play in the National Football League (NFL). Such players include Desmond Howard, Charles Woodson, and Tom Brady. Brady is currently the star **quarterback** for the New England Patriots of the NFL. Perhaps the most famous former University of Michigan football player was Gerald Ford. Ford played **center** and **linebacker** for the Wolverines and later became the president of the United States.

Before Tom Brady became a Super Bowl champion, he was the Michigan Wolverines quarterback. Brady led the Wolverines to victories in the 1999 Citrus Bowl and the 2000 Orange Bowl.

THE OHIO STATE BUCKEYES

For years, Ohio State University's football team has been one of the best in college football. The team, nicknamed the Buckeyes, plays their home games in Ohio Stadium, located in Columbus, Ohio. Each fall, Ohio State fans fill the stadium to watch their favorite team. Fans have been cheering for the Buckeyes since their first game was played in 1890.

The Buckeyes have had many great football teams over the years. One of the best was the 2002 team, which won the national championship. The 2002 championship was the team's seventh in its history. Many NFL players have played for the Buckeyes. Santonio Holmes, A. J. Hawk, and Jake Ballard are just a few former Buckeyes who are currently on an NFL team.

A. J. Hawk was one of the best Ohio State football players of all time. His position was linebacker. Hawk now plays for the Green Bay Packers of the National Football League.

THE EARLY YEARS

The Wolverines **dominated** the early years of the Michigan and Ohio State football rivalry. Michigan won 13 of the first 15 games against Ohio State. The other two games ended in ties. Ohio State finally won a game versus Michigan in 1919. That win was the Buckeyes' first against the Wolverines.

As the years went by, more wins would come for the Buckeyes against the Wolverines. And soon enough the Buckeyes were one of the Wolverine's toughest opponents. One thing was clear, a rivalry had been born. As a result, Michigan and Ohio State would fight it out in many great football games over the years.

Michigan running back Tom Harmon (number 98) runs the ball during a game versus Ohio State in 1939. If you look closely, you'll notice that the players' helmets do not have face masks, as they do today.

THE SNOW BOWL

One of the most famous Michigan and Ohio State football games occurred in 1950. What was most noteworthy about the game was the fact that it was played during a **blizzard**! Despite the snowy and windy weather, nearly 80,000 people turned out to watch the two teams battle. This showed just how popular the Michigan and Ohio State football rivalry had become.

The snow-covered field and fierce winds made it difficult for both teams to play. As a result not too many points were scored in the game. Michigan won the low-scoring game, by a score of 9-3. The game became so famous that college football fans still talk about it today. It is considered one of the best games of the Michigan and Ohio State rivalry.

From the Snow Bowl (top left) to the Rose Bowl: A Michigan victory over Ohio State in the Snow Bowl earned them a spot in the 1951 Rose Bowl, in Pasadena, California.

THE 10-YEAR WAR

Some of the most **competitive** games of the Michigan and Ohio State rivalry occurred between 1969 and 1978. During this time, Michigan won five games, and Ohio State won five games. Michigan and Ohio State each had great football teams during this 10-year span. Each team also had a legendary football coach.

Bo Schembechler was Michigan's football coach. Ohio State was coached by Woody Hayes. Both coaches were among the best coaches in college football. When the well-coached Wolverines and Buckeyes played against each other, their games made for some instant classics!

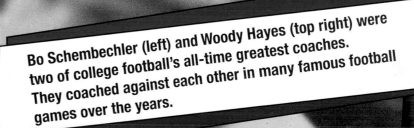

Bo Schembechler (left) and Woody Hayes (top right) were two of college football's all-time greatest coaches. They coached against each other in many famous football games over the years.

THE GAME OF THE CENTURY

One of the best college football games of all time was played between Michigan and Ohio State in 2006. The game was played at Ohio Stadium. At the time, each team had an **undefeated** record of 11-0. Ohio State was ranked number one in the country and Michigan was ranked second.

Ohio State won in a shoot-out, edging Michigan 42-39. The victory earned Ohio State a spot in the national championship game. Had Michigan won the game, they would have likely played for the national championship as well. The game was one of the most heated and competitive games ever played between the teams. The game has become so famous that it is called by many The Game of the Century.

Ohio State quarterback Troy Smith looks downfield as he is being chased by a Michigan defender. In 2006, Smith led the Buckeyes to a 42-39 victory over the Wolverines.

MASCOT TRADITIONS

Have you ever watched an Ohio State football game and spotted a cartoonlike character, with a big round head, cheering on the Buckeyes from the sideline? If so, then you saw Brutus Buckeye. He is the Ohio State football team's **mascot**.

Many college football teams have mascots that are dressed in colorful costumes. One team without such a mascot, however, is the Michigan Wolverines. Instead, Michigan has a real **wolverine** as its mascot. That's right, a real wolverine! Don't worry, though, the wolverine does not run wild around the football stadium. He is kept secure in a cage on the sidelines.

Today the Michigan and Ohio State rivalry is stronger than ever. And as the years go by, many more great games are likely to be played between the Wolverines and Buckeyes.

Brutus Buckeye is all smiles here as he cheers on his favorite college football team. Brutus's head is shaped like a buckeye nut.

WOLVERINE AND BUCKEYE TIMELINE

1950

Michigan defeats Ohio State 9-3 in the Snow Bowl. The victory earns the Wolverines a trip to the 1951 Rose Bowl.

1897

Michigan and Ohio State play their first football game against each other. Michigan wins 34-0.

1969

A period known as the 10-Year War begins with a Michigan victory over Ohio State 24-12.

1997

Michigan wins its eleventh national championship in school history.

1978

The final game of the 10-Year War is played. Michigan wins 14-3. Over the 10-year span, the Wolverines won five games, and the Buckeyes won five games.

2003

The Buckeyes win the national championship by defeating the Miami Hurricanes 31-24 in the Fiesta Bowl. The close game was won by the Bucks in double overtime.

2006

The Buckeyes top the Wolverines 42-39 in a shoot-out at Ohio Stadium. The victory secures a berth for the Buckeyes in the national championship game.

TALE OF THE TAPE

MICHIGAN   OHIO STATE

Ann Arbor, MI	**SCHOOL LOCATION**	Columbus, OH
1817	**UNIVERSITY FOUNDED**	1870
109,901	**STADIUM CAPACITY**	102,329
11	**NATIONAL CHAMPIONSHIPS**	7
3	**HEISMAN WINNERS**	7
Wolverine	**MASCOT**	Brutus Buckeye
Maize and Blue	**SCHOOL COLORS**	Scarlet and Gray

GLOSSARY

ANNUAL (AN-yuh-wul) Something that happens every year.

BLIZZARD (bliz-erd) A heavy snowstorm with strong winds.

CENTER (SEN-ter) The player on a football team who snaps the ball to the quarterback.

COMPETITIVE (kum-pet-i-tiv) Having a strong desire to compete.

CONFERENCE (KON-fer-ens) A group of athletic teams.

DOMINATED (DAH-muh-nayt-ed) Controlled or ruled over a person or a team in a competition.

LINEBACKER (lyn-BA-ker) A player on defense who lines up behind the linemen.

MASCOT (MAS-kot) An animal or person chosen by a group to be their representative or symbol.

NEIGHBORING (NAY-ber-ing) Living near or next to.

QUARTERBACK (KWAHR-ter-bak) A player in football who lines up behind the center and directs the offense.

RIVALRY (RY-vul-ree) Teams that play each other a lot and feel strongly about winning.

UNDEFEATED (un-dih-FEET-ed) Not having lost a competition or game.

WOLVERINE (wuhl-vuh-REEN) A mammal of the northern forest regions that is related to the weasel. Also means a native or resident of Michigan.

INDEX

WEBSITES

Due to the changing nature of Internet links, PowerKids Press has developed an online list of websites related to the subject of this book. This site is updated regularly. Please use this link to access the list:
www.powerkidslinks.com/cfgr/michosu/